By Gary Beck

Novels

Extreme Change
Acts of Defiance
Flawed Connections
Call to Valor
Sudden Conflicts
Crumbling Ramparts
Flare Up
Raise High the Walls
Still Defiant
State of Rage
Wave Length
Protective Agency
Obsess
Still Obsessed
Rescue Me
Until the Bell

Poetry

Expectations
Days of Destruction
Dawn in Cities
Assault on Nature
Songs of a Clerk
Civilized Ways
Conditioned Response
Displays
Perceptions
Fault Lines
Tremors
Unillumined
Perturbations
Blossoms of Decay
Rude Awakenings
Blunt Force
Remission of Order
Contusions
Transitions
Earth Links
Mortal Coil
Desperate Seeker
Too Harsh For Pastels
Temporal Dreams
Severance
Redemption Value
Fractional Disorder
Disruptions
Ignition Point
Learning Curve
Resonance
Turbulence
Lacerations
State of the Union
Purpose
Double Envelopment
Unveilings
Discoveries
Molecular Distortion
Virtual Living

Play Collections & Plays

The Big Match and other one act plays
Collected Plays of Gary Beck Volume I
Plays of Aristophanes translated then directed by Gary Beck
Collected Plays of Gary Beck Volume II
Four Plays of Moliere translated then directed by Gary Beck
Collected Plays of Gary Beck Volume III
Sophocles – Three Plays
Agamemnon

Short Story Collections

A Glimpse of Youth and other stories
Now I Accuse and other stories
Dogs Don't Send Flowers and other stories
Judgments and other stories

Essays

The Republic of Dreams and other essays
Collected Essays of Gary Beck

Virtual Living

by

Gary Beck

ISBN: 978-81-19654-44-4

First Edition: 2024
Rs. 200/-

Cyberwit.net
HIG 45 Kaushambi Kunj, Kalindipuram
Allahabad - 211011 (U.P.) India
http://www.cyberwit.net
Tel: +(91) 9415091004
E-mail: info@cyberwit.net

Printed at Repro India Limited.

To Tom Sheehan,
whose vitality is a bright light
that refuses to flicker or die out.

C'est de souffrance et de bonté
Que sera fait la beauté.

Les Collines

Guillaume Apollinaire

Poems from 'Virtual Living' have been published by:

Writing Knights Press, Torrid Literature Journal, Poetry Pacific, Poetry Life & Times, Madswirl, Pyrokinection, Kind of a Hurricane Press,, En Pointe Magazine, East Coast Literary Review, Boston Poetry Magazine, Ascent Aspirations Magazine, Electric Rather Literary Magazine, The Poets Haven, The Angry Manifesto, mgversion2datura, Random Poem Tree, Polseguera, Coldnoon Travel Poetics, Intentional Walk (Sundress Publications), Nous Magazine and The Remembered Arts Journal.

'Escape to Cyberspace and other poems, a chapbook from the collection 'Virtual Living' was published by Writing Knights Press.

.

Contents

Poems from 'Virtual Living' have been published by: 6
Mindscape 11
Birdsong 12
Sports Fans 13
Distraction 15
Avatars 16
Senior Search 17
Future War 18
Trace of Life 19
Nothing Changes 20
Gaming 21
Withdrawal Symptoms 22
Remote Attacks 23
Different Worlds 24
Escape to Cyberspace 26
Tenure 27
Natural Activity 28
Sensory Experience 29
Economic Change 30
Sports Fans II 31
Confused Values 33
Individualism 34
Techno-State 35
Gaming II 36
Observation 37
Afghani 38
Thermodynamics 39
Choices 40
Future War II 41
Focus 42
Desynthesis 43

Intent 44
Internet Services 45
Exposition 46
Sports Fans III 47
Inmate 48
Historical Recurrence 49
Accommodation 50
Future War III 51
Captive Audiences 52
Unrest 53
The Vista of History 54
Gaming III 55
Reportage 56
Purpose 57
Detached Observers 58
Web Life 59
Duty 60
Identification 61
Globalization 62
Sports Fans IV 63
Motives 64
Narcissism 65
Hibernators 66
Surfing for Sex 67
Gaming IV 68
Hacking 69
Revolt in the Desert 70
Telephone Dating 71
Digital Escape 72
Deception 73
Cyber Punks 74
User's Risk 75
Love At First Kill 76
Learning Process 77
Make Believe 78

Future War IV ... 79
Earthlink ... 80
Forecast ... 81
Forward force ... 82
Sports Fan V ... 83
Death In Our Time ... 84
Disguise ... 85
Duality ... 86
Toilers ... 87
Digital Virtue ... 88
Gaming V ... 89
Mass Transit ... 90
Deluded Bureaucrats ... 91
Distract and Conquer ... 92
Users ... 93
Does Crime Pay? ... 94
Recession ... 95
Castles in the Sky ... 96
Future War V ... 97
Viewers ... 98
For Whom the Web Trolls ... 99
Compulsion ... 100
Hyper Torpor ... 101
Vacations ... 102
Flagging Efforts ... 103
Gaming VI ... 104
Web Contact ... 105
Out There ... 106
Malicious Dolts ... 108
Love Search ... 109
Spy Tech ... 110
Philosophy ... 111
Sudden Surprise ... 112
Counter Attack ... 113
Fantasy Football ... 114
Cyber War ... 115

Mindscape

Dreams shatter,
more fragile
than steel, brick, glass
man-made materials,
confining spaces
for the mental container
of hopes, fears, guilt,
unlike other animals
whose sleep exertions
re-enact
feeding, flight.

Birdsong

The closer the highway
the closer to death,
so build your nest
as far as you can
from works of man.

Sports Fans

High school students cheer
at the top of their lungs
for their football team,
unaware of
the math student
ignored by all
who may build the future,
while former sport's heroes
dwell in the past,
unable to forget
earlier glory.

College students root
for the home team,
eager to belong
to a bigger world,
paint their faces
in school colors,
identifying with
an institution
encouraging sports
more than science,
relegating the brightest
to unrequited dreams
of supple cheerleaders.

Many football fans
either yearn for the past,
or never grew up.

Some fear the future,
apprehensive of
the loss of function,
try to belong,
rooting for their team.
Others don't realize
pros are as distant
as movie stars,
except they hurt each other
for large salaries,
while loyal fans
wear stupid hats,
wave witless signs,
scream for victory
for favorite teams.

Distraction

People walk the streets
text messaging,
thumbs urgent
to communicate,
no longer linked
to cell phones,
instead enslaved
by tiny screens
that never warn
of approaching danger.

Avatars

Electronic escape
to an easier world
allows participants
to play make believe,
just more sophisticated
than childhood games.

There is no danger
except to ego
when the avatar
is unsuccessful
on the playing fields
of fantasy land.

Lucretius said
atoms and void
make up the universe.
Those who escape
to artificial worlds
display their share
of vacuum.

Senior Search

The refusal to be
left behind
propels seniors
to the internet,
seeking companionship,
friendship, romance,
other benefits,
hoping to avoid
surfing predators
cruising the web
searching for the lonely,
the vulnerable.

Future War

Cyber warriors
defend the nation
from sneak attack
seated comfortably
at computer screens,
never face an enemy,
never draw blood,
will never know
traditional battlefields,
yet are as vital
as combat troops,
though not regarded
heroically.

Trace of Life

I do not rise.
I do not fall.
Am nourished
artificially,
tubular feeding
on I know not what,
chemicals in,
waste out,
hint of sentience
flickering eyes
responsive to tv,
courtesy of
remote sponsors.

Nothing Changes

The Circus Maximus
in ancient Rome
entertained the masses
with bloody spectacles,
distribution of bread
temporarily sating
ravenous appetites.
After the show
citizens and slaves
went home together
to usual conditions,
luxury for some,
suffering for most.
The gift of television
entertains all,
especially the poor
shown over and over
goods and services
they cannot have,
except by becoming
career athletes, criminals.

Gaming

Video gamers
urgent to compete,
inadequate
to challenges
of the real world,
strive to win
artificial acclaim
on safe screens.

Withdrawal Symptoms

Jane Doe works at home,
consumer research,
uses the computer
for virtually everything.
Pays rent online,
talks to friends online,
orders meals online,
even has sex online.
Jane Doe's life,
the wave of the future,
unless we lose
power supply.

Remote Attacks

Kids who grew up
playing video games
controlled by joysticks
now remotely pilot drones
from comfortable seats
removed from the dangers
of distant battlefields,
targeting enemies
in Afghanistan, Pakistan,
with surprise attacks
that kill efficiently,
their only combat hazard
finger cramping
before their shift ends,
when they return
to secure quarters
somewhere in America,
far from the enemy.

Different Worlds

The soldier slowly walks
a dusty village street,
senses on full alert,
tense with expectation
of Taliban attack.

The gamer tightly grips
the complex controller
that guides his avatar
on an alien planet,
where monsters lurk.

The soldier sweats with fear
of explosive devices
that he cannot see,
but painfully learned
eagerly await him.

The gamer struts boldly,
immune to emotion,
ready to fire his blaster
at alien creatures
waiting in ambush.

Soldiers only relax
when they return safely
to a semi-secure base,
another mission survived
in Indian country.

Gamers reach for a beer,
elated with high score,
enemies slaughtered,
avatar safely stored
when the game is over.

Escape to Cyberspace

Online allurements
attract more and more users
who abandon newspapers,
magazines, television,
connect to anything desired,
play virtual games
secure in an avatar
that gives vicarious thrills
in internet indulgence,
completely protected
from danger, disease.

Tenure

Inhabitants of palaces
never recover
from shock of eviction,
even when comforted
by cash in Swiss banks,
spending their days
yearning for past grandeur,
unable to accept
the loss of power.

Natural Activity

Birds do not live
vicariously,
busy all day
gathering food,
never hang out
playing video games,
waste time twittering,
except bird talk,
sit up all night
in front of a screen,
but go to sleep
as soon as it's dark
in the comforting nest.

Sensory Experience

Radio once compelled us
to pay attention
to what we heard
and listen carefully.
Movies isolated us
as we sat alone in darkness,
rapturously glued
to the silver screen.
TV chained us at home
watching the revealed world,
a paltry substitute
for imagination.
The internet erased
international boundaries,
allowing users
world wide exploration
anonymously,
mostly for trivia,
sometimes for science,
too often for evil,
unleashing new dangers
on the unprepared world.

Economic Change

We used to go to the bank
to deposit money,
greeted by tellers
courteous, pleasant,
who made it easier
to accept low interest
on hard-earned wages.
Now we bank online
with no consolation
for meager returns,
automated service.

Sports Fans II

High school fencing
deludes youngsters
nurtured by Hollywood,
dreaming
swashbuckling sword fights.
Most fade away
bored by conventions
of the foil.
Family and friends
attend the matches,
cheer lustily
to make up for
the tiny crowd.

College fencers,
mostly math majors,
engineering students,
train hard,
after the first year
choose saber or epée,
become specialists
in a weapon,
some demonstrate
real talent.
Family and friends,
perhaps a girl friend,
attend the matches,
applaud politely
for a good bout.

Olympic fencers
are world-class athletes
who might survive
a deadly duel.
Family and friends,
ex-fencers
on their first bellies,
second wives,
attend the matches,
grumbling about
how good they could have been,
if only....

Confused Values

Parents urge children
to compete in sports,
demonstrate talent,
be recognized,
get wealth, fame, acclaim,
while our misguided land,
deceived with material things,
completely ignores
gifts for math, science,
unappreciated by those
equating worth
with rich rewards.

Individualism

The Information Age
allows us to march
to the beat of a different drum,
as long as we purchase
the same goods and services
as everyone else.

Techno-State

Citizens far removed
from survival demands
spend more time twittering
than hunting, gathering,
tilling the soil, producing
sustenance for the nation,
inventions that preserve
the endangered future.
They speak a new language,
short, abbreviated,
engaging most users
in mindless chatter,
reminiscent
of monkey jabber
leading some to question
evolution.

Gaming II

Electronic devices
morally encourage
brutal carnage
by armchair warriors
remotely immune
from blood, gore, death,
who battle furiously
and only retreat
from seats of safety
when the game ends.

Observation

The Earth always simmered
with ongoing warfare
made remote by distance,
except for participants.
Electronic news
rushes to deliver
blood, gore, death,
to eager viewers
well protected
from harsh reality
by tv and computer screens.

Afghani

I prostrate myself
five times daily,
recite the prayers,
invoke Allah
who never answers,
while the Taliban,
western infidels,
corrupt governors,
demand my taxes,
the Americans
pressure me
not to grow poppy.
It is easier to take
my AK-47,
go to the mountains,
kill whoever
offers less money.
Allah be praised.

Thermodynamics

Motion
creates ambiguities,
determines destinations,
maintaining
application of energy
seeking expansion,
contraction,
indifferent
to human needs
for conservation.

Choices

Bodies swirl through cities
divorced from evolution
suspending genetic progress,
fattening themselves
on chemical produce
dissolving structure,
completely conceding
future sustenance
for urban comforts.

Future War II

General ---__________
wanted his cyber troops
to fully experience
the feel of battle,
so his programmers
added a sound track
of gunfire and explosions
to the normally silent
computer searches.
The unseen weapons of tomorrow
may win or lose a war
in electronic conflict
that might not be noticed
until we're defeated.

Focus

Energy bursts,
natural, synthetic,
accelerate effort,
prevent interception
by velocity.
Considerations
moral, ethical,
undispersed
interrupt targets,
disrupt intentions
of acquisition.

Desynthesis

People must think
that oxygen
grows on buildings,
since we replace trees
with lifeless structures.
Soon we'll suffer
rude awakening
when carbon emissions,
unabsorbed by
glass, steel, concrete,
asphyxiate us.

Intent

Objectives,
often interrupted
by circumstance,
complications,
frequently require
structural support,
or resolution
may be disrupted,
thwarting conclusions.

Internet Services

Cybersex
may vex
concerned moms,
prudish wives,
jealous lovers,
social moralists,
but junior,
hubby,
boy friend,
assorted creeps,
won't catch disease
from small screens.

Exposition

Cities breed illusions,
safety, security,
compelling abdication
of traditional instincts
that once facilitated
hunting, gathering,
agriculture,
survival,
arbitrarily substituting
supermarkets,
cell phone stores,
nail salons,
creating nothing,
reducing paper
to electronic transmissions
requiring devotion
to screens of diversion,
replicating reality.

Sports Fans III

Aging gamers
unwilling, unable
to sweat and strain
for sports skills
needed to compete,
whoop and holler
with superficial pleasure
at artificial victories
on virtual playing fields.

Inmate

I sit on prison sofa
transfixed
by entertainment center,
totally absorbed
in electronic programming
transmitting confinement
without hope of parole.

Historical Recurrence

Fractured states
invariably corrupted
by special interests
shatter under pressure
from bitter conflict,
ethnic, racial, religious,
impelled by guns
towards extermination,
eliminating
hope of mediation,
beyond agreement,
destruction preferred
to compromise.

Accommodation

Permanence,
a mild delusion
for millennia
of insecure
human expectations
doomed by nature
that compels vacating
short-term housing.

Future War III

The children we yelled at
for neglecting homework,
playing video games,
are grown up now,
busy controlling
pilotless drones
that attack Al Qaeda,
the Taliban,
other enemies
thousands of miles away.
Let's hope they're more mature
than the careless kids
they used to be,
who have been given
power of life and death.

Captive Audiences

Securely perched
in front of tv,
future concerns
totally erased
electronically,
direct transmissions
of subtle commandments
to sit back,
do nothing,
anesthetizes viewers.

Unrest

Dissatisfied citizens
in lands of oppression
take to the streets,
surprising their masters
with sudden outbursts
of popular protest,
aided and abetted
by technology,
facebook, twitter,
sending out the word
for demonstrations,
threatening the rule
of aging tyrants.

The Vista of History

Civilizations
rise, fall
mostly led
by urgent men
obsessed by appetites
for power, possessions,
unconcerned
with those they consume
in the age old quest
for domination.

Gaming III

Gamblers gather
in welcoming casinos
lusting their money
in controlled environments
eliminating
night, day, time,
carefully designed
to always insure
visitors leave poorer
than when they arrived.

Reportage

Tv news
pokes its muzzle
anywhere
anytime,
suctioning
violent material
indiscriminately,
war, terror,
gruesome murders,
titillating viewers,
keeping them glued
to comfortable seats,
watching the suffering
of distant victims.

Purpose

Globalization aspires
to equip the world
electronically
with screens of acquisition,
slickly displaying
what we can obtain,
as long as we remain
obedient consumers.

Detached Observers

The Roman Empire collapsed
succumbing to the onslaught
of barbarian hordes,
while isolated monks
in secure monasteries
preserved the heritage
of civilization.
As America declines
dwellers in ivory towers,
electronic custodians
of human knowledge,
cannot conceive
there is no protection
in accessible colleges
from social disorder.

Web Life

Social networking
a constant
in the information age,
a digital distraction
that disrupts abilities
to use the brain properly,
does not deter users
from frequently connecting
to unproductive sites.

Duty

In the age old contract
between soldier and state,
the soldier does his duty
to preserve the homeland,
the state protects the rights
of the absent warrior.
If the state betrays the soldier
by oppressing his family
the covenant is broken,
the soldier's obligation
to shed blood in battle
for an ungrateful nation
may not be relied on.

Identification

In ancient times
winning or losing
brutal battles
often determined
survival of a people.
Olympic games
were introduced
to divert the masses
from frequent crises,
reward the victors
without bloodshed.
Modern entertainment
streamed non-stop on tv,
the internet,
provides distraction,
substitutes spectation
for needed action.

Globalization

Cities expand
across the globe
devouring the land,
covering the earth
with strangling concrete,
training the people
in urban existence
to become alike
in wealth or poverty,
as the rich flourish,
the poor suffer,
both increasingly unfit
to survive nature's extremes.

Sports Fans IV

Passionate viewers
unable to compete
gather in sports bars,
gather in livingrooms,
watch the home team,
drink, cheer, yell
for their favorite's success,
vitally concerned with winning,
much more important
than love of the game,
appreciation
for loser's efforts.

Motives

Tennis parents,
well-to-do,
upscale aspiring,
drive their children
to excel,
pushing, cajoling,
threatening,
any means necessary,
compelling
pliant offspring
to achieve success,
satisfy vicariously
Mom and Dad
identified with
offspring's accomplishments,
fantasizing
fame, fortune,
championships
no matter the cost
to their offspring.

Narcissism

A growing malady
of teens, adults,
who love themselves
more than ever before,
obsessed with I, me,
forgetting us, we.
Poets are victims
of our self-absorbed times,
apparently renouncing
positive emotions,
often substituting
anger-related words
in resentful refrains,
bitter complaints
of injuries sustained
in an unheeding world.

Hibernators

Urban warriors
go to battle
electronically,
safe behind the screens
of various devices,
pushing buttons,
moving joysticks,
spectating,
ordering takeout,
any pretext
to remain indoors.

Surfing for Sex

Neural principles
of higher cognitive functions,
display the same limitations
intellectually
in sexual behavior,
as in the rest of existence.
Electronic search
for gratification
reveals the secrets
of millions of men
accessing online porn,
obvious indication
of unfulfilled desires,
domestic dissatisfaction.

Gaming IV

The roulette wheel spins,
cards are dealt,
dice are rolled,
faster ways to lose
than voracious slots
devouring cash,
consuming players.

Hacking

Hackers intrude
into government sites
completely concealed
behind protective screens,
disrupt services,
steal information,
destroy functions,
generally convinced
they will not be discovered
and we will never learn
if they are clever show-offs,
cyber warriors,
malicious trolls.

Revolt in the Desert

After years of abuse
by harsh dictators
arabs reached for cellphones,
dialed into twitter,
called their countrymen
with a summons to protest.
Citizens gathered
in the public square
demanding change,
despite orders to disperse
by security forces
loyal to the government,
as long as they were paid.
Determined people
refused to obey,
compelled corrupt leaders
to flee the country,
a notable triumph
of social networking.

Telephone Dating

Tv ads entice
the lonely, the shy,
social misfits
who can't cope
with face to face
personal meetings.
Instead the vulnerable
talk to strangers
who seem pleasant,
but may lure the caller
to a chamber of horrors.

Digital Escape

Intellectual snobs
disdain people
in two groups;
those who sit home
watching big screen tv
rooted in front of the set,
others who surf the net
shopping, reading, chatting, sexting,
more actively engaged
than passive spectation,
but sometimes interact,
however condescendingly,
when they happen to meet
on the world wide web.

Deception

A teen age girl
made new friends
in an on-line chat room
supposed to be for teens.
She and another girl
found much in common,
had private chats,
decided to meet
at a local mall.
Instead of the girl,
a scary man approached,
claimed to be the girl's father,
tried to persuade her
to come to their house.
The girl was smart enough
to refuse to go,
but not smart enough
to call the police.
She returned that night
to the same chat room
that might have led
to fatal encounter.

Cyber Punks

Electronic bullies
sneak around the web
until they discover
targets of opportunity,
assaulting the unwary
with nasty harassment,
petty threats, sick abuses,
skulking behind screens
shielded from capture,
anonymously protected
by the constitution
with freedom of expression
that allows them to persecute
innocent victims,
escape punishment.

User's Risk

Online games
addict people,
make them belligerent,
distract from reality,
leave them empty,
trapped in delusion
that virtual worlds
are a substitute
for this demanding life.

Love At First Kill

Fantasy game players
on the World of Warcraft
kill a yellow-eyed demon,
then let their avatars
explore exotic landscapes
where they meet others
with instant messaging,
chat, get acquainted,
find out to their surprise
they're on a date
that leads to romance,
develops a relationship,
culminates in marriage,
a triumph of human feelings
over the anonymity
of cyberspace.

Learning Process

Search engines,
online databases,
make people unlikely
to remember information
that comes too easily
to be retained,
as long as computers
contain our knowledge
continue to function.

Make Believe

A child's game,
inventive,
entertaining,
now transformed
by immature grown-ups
hiding inadequacy
in electronic escape
to virtual reality.

Future War IV

Video games
train our youth
with quick eyes,
quick hands,
to kill the enemy,
exterminate him
without real bloodshed,
casualties,
consequences,
(except late for school).
They join the army
ready to launch
a destructive shower
of hi-tech missiles,
without moral qualms,
on designated targets.

Earthlink

Nature
is under global assault,
slashed and stabbed
by ravishers,
as mortal dwellers
loot and pillage,
brutally besiege
our only habitat
of continuation.

Forecast

Atmospheric conditions
progressively decompose
breathable air,
so city dwellers
move indoors,
underground,
forced to utilize
pictures of the past,
blue skies,
green trees,
colorful flowers,
artificial sweeteners
for confined exiles.
Thrust

Forward force

impells
receptive bodies
to lift remote,
controller,
other device,
accomplishment
of minimal value,
substituting diversion
for action,
haphazardly dwindling
meaningful tomorrows.

Sports Fan V

Adults, children
wear sports shirts
of favorite players,
names on front,
numbers on back,
proclaiming to the world
loyal support
for their heroes,
normal in children
inexperienced in values,
immature in adults
who should know better
than selecting
superficial figures
for emulation.

Death In Our Time

The loss of loved ones,
made bearable
by technology,
gives comfort
with tv, texting,
softening
pain of passing.

Disguise

Technical progress
caters to escape
from harsh reality,
kindly creating
enhancing avatars
completely concealing
inadequacies,
cleverly hidden
artificially
in false personae.

Duality

America exists
one way for the rich
another for the poor
who have in common
leveling tv,
available to all,
so servants can watch
the same shows as masters
and spectate
desirable goods,
limited to some
in the unjust
lottery of life.

Toilers

Humble citizens
have little say
in the fate of nations
as long as conditions
are tolerable,
leaving the future
in the hands of others.
When things go wrong
outraged populations
sometimes stir to action,
confront the rulers,
disrupt tyranny.

Digital Virtue

Righteous hackers
declared cyberwar
on the city of Orlando,
as punishment for arresting
an anti-poverty group
feeding the homeless.
The poor embarrass
Disneyland tourists,
so ordinances were passed
to keep them off the streets.
Denial-of-service attacks
overwhelmed a website,
knocked it offline,
which disrupted the city
that rejected a truce
with the hackers,
preferring to hide
the poor from the public.

Gaming V

Electronic devices
multiply opportunity
for effete competition
completely unreliant
on physical prowess,
no risk of injury,
only humiliation
for ignominious defeat
on smirking screens.

Mass Transit

New York City subways
soon will dispense
with human personnel,
engineers, conductors,
even station agents,
until the system
is automated.
Yet in the absence of people
there will be no robots
to provide assistance
in case of emergency
in underground travel.

Deluded Bureaucrats

New York City officials
wanted to make the streets
bike-user friendly,
discourage autos
that congest, pollute,
and built bike lanes
to encourage pedalers,
but made drastic cuts
in public transportation,
with the foolish idea
that two wheels
would replace four.

Distract and Conquer

The rulers of our land
cheerfully encourage
social networking,
cynically believing
we will be too busy
chatting with strangers
on twitter, facebook,
to pay attention
to issues of our time
that allow the rich
to become richer,
while the rest of us
get less and less.

Users

Capital accumulates
faster for the rich,
historically abler
to manipulate
means of production,
exploitation of labor,
government regulations,
to secure more profit
at the expense of the public.

Does Crime Pay?

Perpetrators
of unlawful acts
frequently escape
the wheel of justice,
our complex system
almost overwhelmed
by illicit hordes,
forcing tolerance
of many crimes,
now acceptable
to a weary public.

Recession

You try to earn a living
in the Information Age,
acquire goods, services
that benefit your family.
You don't exploit others,
want to be comfortable
while the poor get poorer,
try to control the fears
of leaving the middle class
submerging to poverty,
as the rich covet more,
willing to use any means
to increase their wealth,
despite how they infect
our ailing nation.

Castles in the Sky

Millions make the daily trek
to local stores
for lottery tickets,
ignoring the odds
that allow winning
for only a few,
as they seek
the valid passport
to the land of dreams,
the elusive payoff.

Future War V

Push button warfare,
joystick combat,
doesn't require
face to face conflict
with bloodthirsty foes
by armchair warriors
who see the battlefield
through tv cameras
on pilotless drones
that hover for hours
and identify
opportune targets,
yet operators
sometimes confuse
fighters with civilians,
but zap them anyway.

Viewers

Remote from danger
they change the channel
from dreadful images
of Japan's despair
ravaged by tsunamis,
tainted with radiation
that will poison others,
and seek lighter fare
of mindless entertainment,
rather than depressing
daily news.

For Whom the Web Trolls

Abusers of the web's
anonymous openness
assault who they choose
electronically,
persecuting, embarrassing
helpless targets
with revealing photos,
indiscreet comments,
insulting remarks,
maliciously posted
for public consumption,
often harming
innocent victims.

Compulsion

Casinos hum, buzz, ring,
shriek with moans of despair,
brief cries of elation,
as humans, machines
combine relentlessly
to collect money
from desperate gamblers,
obsessively trapped
in the endless quest
for the big jackpot.

Hyper Torpor

Compared to tv,
internet activity
requires attention
to data, messages, games,
engaging briefly
moderate intelligence,
distinctly different
from mindless spectation.

Vacations

Cruise ships sail
from northern cities
to tropic isles
where eager natives
welcome passengers
who rush ashore
overburdened with money
shop, gape, drink too much,
buy cheap souvenirs,
return aboard
weary, but ready
for more drinks, meals,
scheduled recreation,
then the next isle.
Tourist sightseeing
begins to pall,
finds consolation
in shuffleboard,
socializing,
dancing the night away,
constant activity
until the last port.

Flagging Efforts

Flags of a country
symbolize the spirit
that makes up a nation,
proudly flown by armies
government buildings,
patriotic households
displaying belief
in the land they love.
Rabid sports fans
with confused values
wave their banners
for professional athletes
competing for money,
not national interests.

Gaming VI

Gamblers used to go
to glamorous casinos
and try their luck
against human dealers.
Although the house always won
they found consolation
in scantily clad girls
serving free drinks, free meals.
Now gamblers play online,
lose their money
in the comfort of home,
without services,
or the faintest idea
if the game is honest.

Web Contact

People spend their time
seeking friends on the internet,
sending short messages
requesting brief exchanges
they hope will lead
to deeper relationships.
Protected behind remote screens,
they approach strangers
naïve in expectations
that they will not meet
sexual predators.

Out There

Personal faults
are quickly confessed
on facebook, twitter,
by peculiar people
seeking an audience,
rushing to display
inappropriate acts,
revelations
spreading faster
than jungle drums,
smoke signals,
flashing mirrors,
until everyone knows
what they did wrong.

Electronic Egypt

Years of oppression,
civil rights abuses,
endemic poverty
finally boiled over
as the disenfranchised
rushed to cellphones,
roused their neighbors
in peaceful protest
that grew and grew
the more violence
they confronted,
as social networking
toppled a government
of obsolete leaders.

Malicious Dolts

In fairy tales,
children's songs,
trolls lurked under bridges,
only a menace
to unwary travelers.
Nowadays
they cruise The Web
causing mischief,
misery, suffering,
from seats of safety
behind anonymous screens,
cruelly launching
vicious attacks
on the vulnerable,
smug they avoid
retribution.

Love Search

A lonely young man
met a girl online
and gradually built
a romantic dream.
Their relationship grew
more personal, intense,
and they decided to meet.
The man was shocked
when instead of the girl
an older woman appeared,
who turned out to be
the girl's fifty year old mother.

Spy Tech

The fly on the wall
may really be a drone,
a miniature bug
with audio, video
capability,
that monitors
secret conversations,
views maps, documents,
except in sterile rooms
that forbid insects.

Philosophy

I thought once
how Socrates would sit
in the marketplace
of ancient Athens,
questioning passersby
on the nature of life,
confounding the arrogant,
dismissing the foolish,
ignoring the slaves,
alienating most citizens,
while Sparta relentlessly
devoured the Empire.

Sudden Surprise

Terrorists travel
under the watchful eyes
of hi-tech satellites
only discovering
in final moments
as missiles hit,
that their efforts
to avoid surveillance
were in vain.

Counter Attack

Supporters of the regime
assaulted the protesters
demanding change.
Mounted on horses, camels,
hirelings of the state
tried to suppress
legitimate dissent
with brutal violence.
Peaceful citizens
social networking,
reached for cellphones
instead of weapons,
rallied the people,
resisted tyranny.

Fantasy Football

Non-mature men
gather together
for role playing
as coaches, owners
of professional teams,
they do not own, control,
buy, sell, trade
members of their teams
finding satisfaction
in imaginary games.

Cyber War

Generals complain
the unseen foe
strikes sneakily
at vulnerable targets,
power grids, waterworks,
transportation hubs,
commercial markets,
unfairly ignoring
the rules of war,
conveniently forgetting
their own innovations,
subversive attacks
with rockets, missiles,
pilotless drones,
helicopter assaults,
other violations
of formal battlefields.

www.ingramcontent.com/pod-product-compliance
Lightning Source LLC
Chambersburg PA
CBHW022158160726
48282CB00024B/243
* 9 7 8 8 1 1 9 6 5 4 4 4 4 *